MORE PRACTICE, BETTER RESULTS!

The Bagpipe Tutorial app for your daily exercises

- more than 250 instruction videos, shown in variable speeds
- covers all tunes from the Bagpipe Tutorial book
- more than 100 embellishment exercises
- full app functionality available offline
- available in 3 languages (English, French & German)

TEST FOR FREE!

LIGHT VERSION app for free with a few videos & exercises

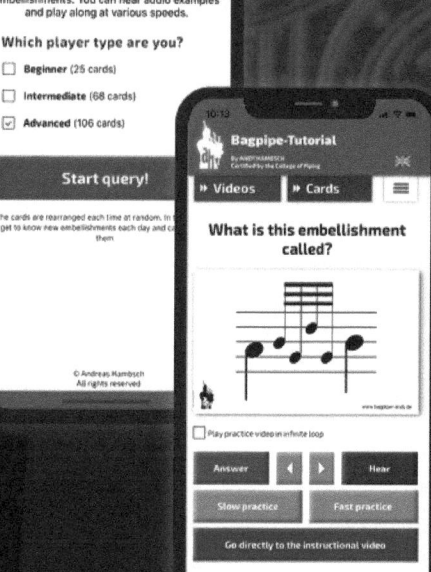

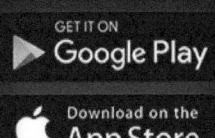

© Andreas Hambsch

"Good music comes from the heart of the musician and lives in the hearts of the listening audience"

(- Bagpipe School -)

Learn the Highland Bagpipe

first steps for absolute beginners

All Grace Notes & Embellishments

Publisher

"printed and published by BoD - Books on Demand, Norderstedt"

BOD – Books on Demand GmbH
ISBN 978-3-74-128558-5

1th Edition 2023
English

Copyright © bagpipe-tutorial.com, Donald MacLeod

Web
www.bagpipe-tutorial.com

E-mail
info@bagpipe-tutorial.com

Cover/Photos – Bagpipe-Tutorial
Contents/Text – Bagpipe Tutorial

Learn the Highland Bagpipe - first steps for absolute beginners

Bagpipe Tutorial App

available on the App Store

About the Bagpipe Tutorial App: Recommended by the best pipers in the world!

This tutorial app is the most comprehensive multimedia reference in the world on playing the Scottish bagpipes. It contains more than 250 videos demonstrating control of the instrument and finger techniques, including audio-visual information on all the grace notes and embellishments. Numerous exercises convey the essentials of Scottish piping.

Once the app is installed, you have access to all of its functions and all the videos, even in offline mode. The tutorial is ideal for absolute beginners up to advanced pipers and can be used for independent study or as a source of examples for lessons. Its aim is to give the student basic information about the instrument, a solid foundation in technique and expert guidance on the route to becoming an accomplished piper.

This tutorial app by Donald MacLeod is a milestone in the teaching of the Scottish bagpipes. Easily understandable and thorough, it is a worthwhile investment for anyone interested in piping. The Bagpipe Tutorial book, also by Donald MacLeod, is an ideal supplement.

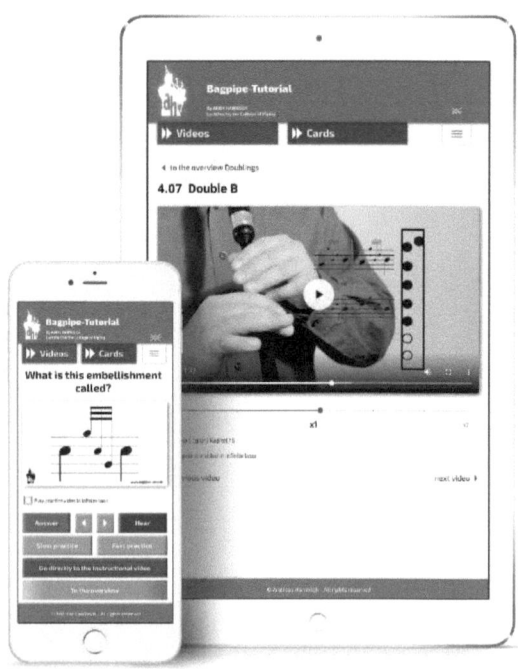

Learn the Highland Bagpipe - first steps for absolute beginners

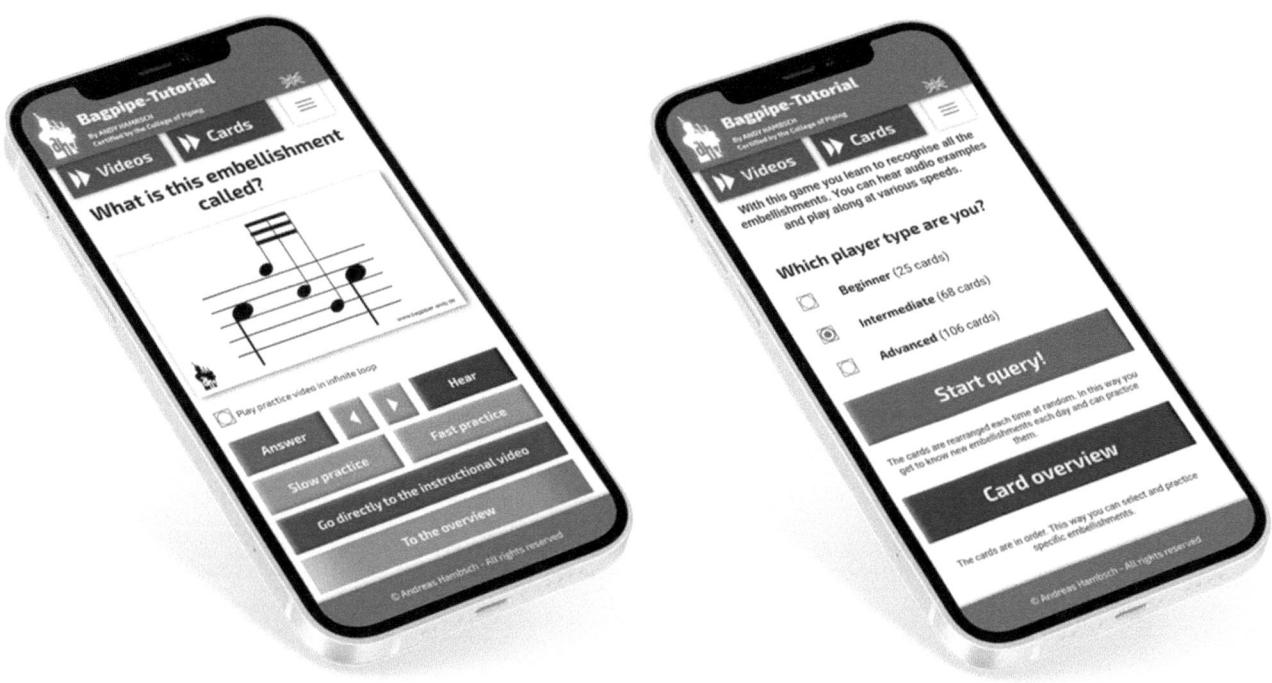

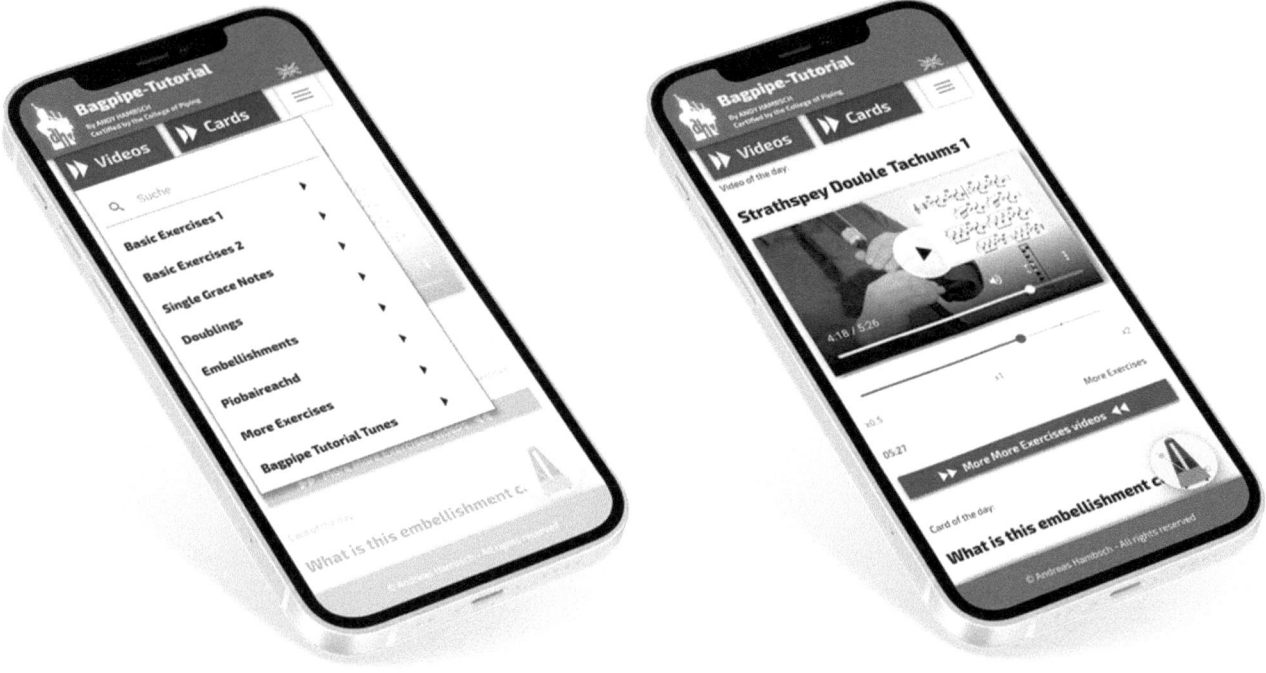

What you need

A practice chanter

and

the Bagpipe Tutorial book

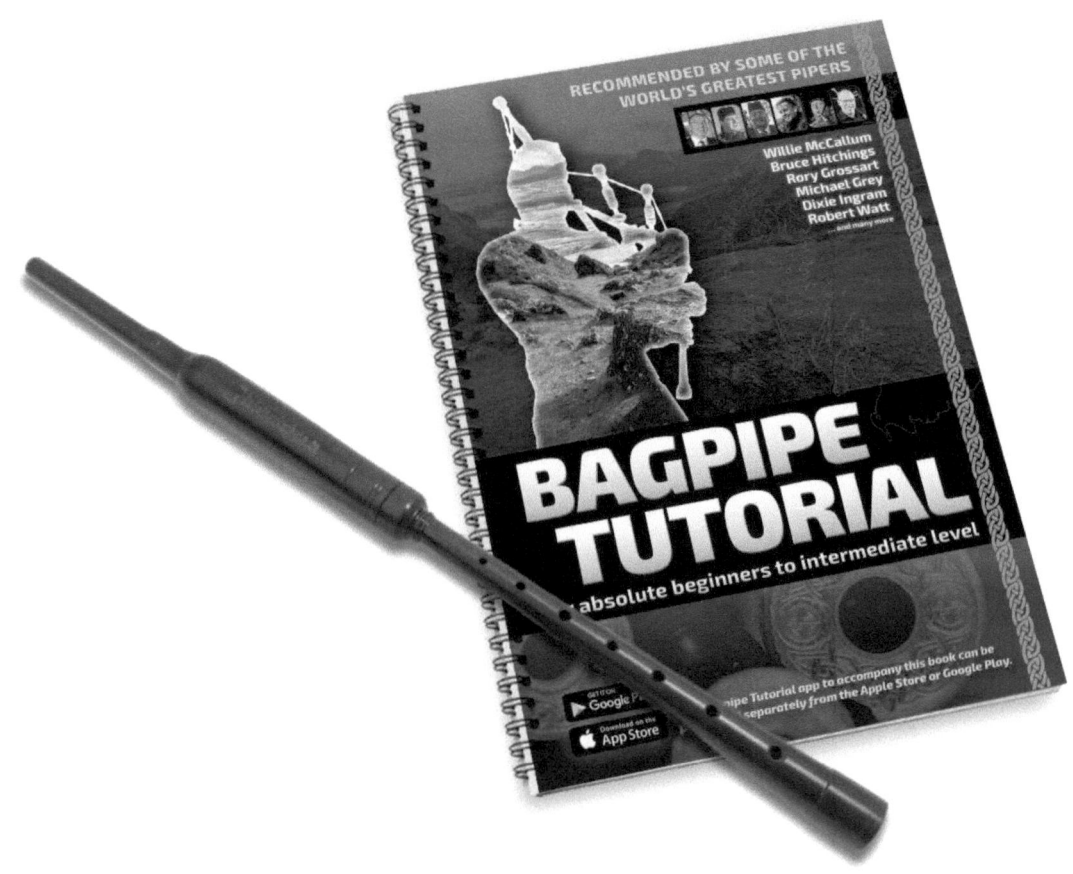

Available from Amazon or www.bagpipe-tutorial.com

Learn the Highland Bagpipe - first steps for absolute beginners

Fingering Table

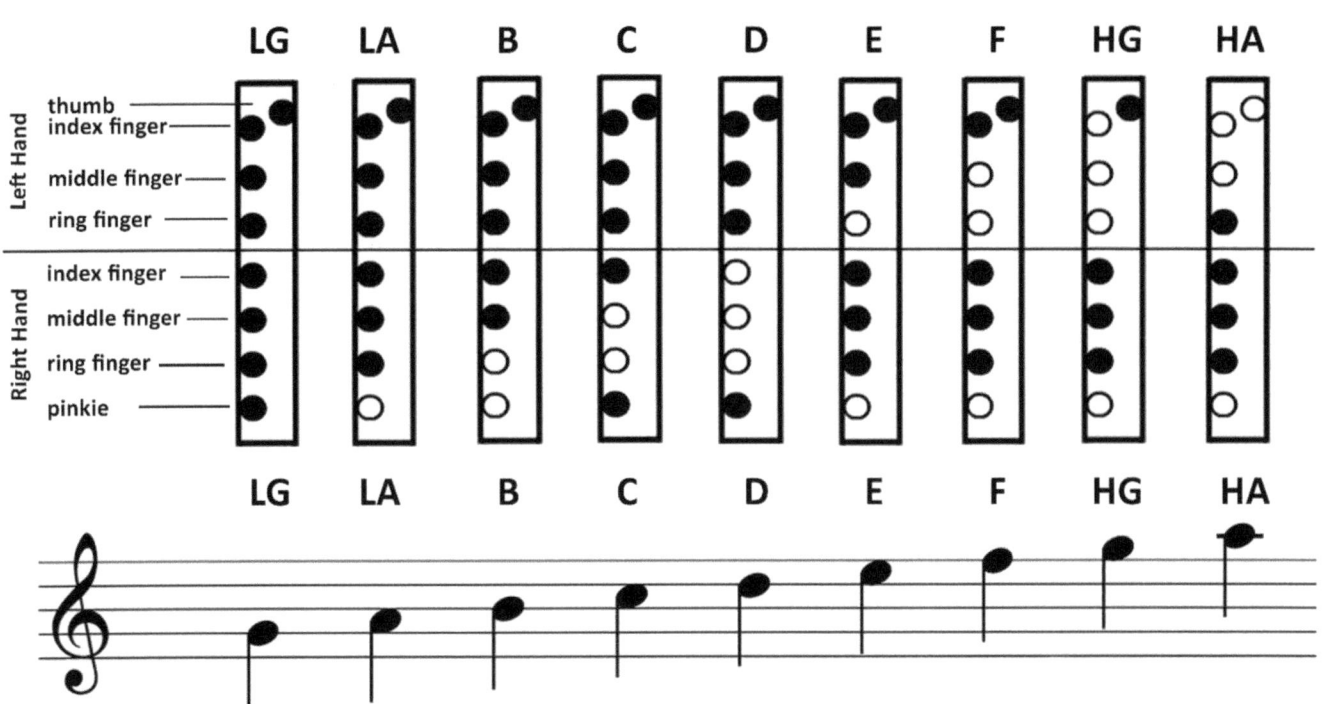

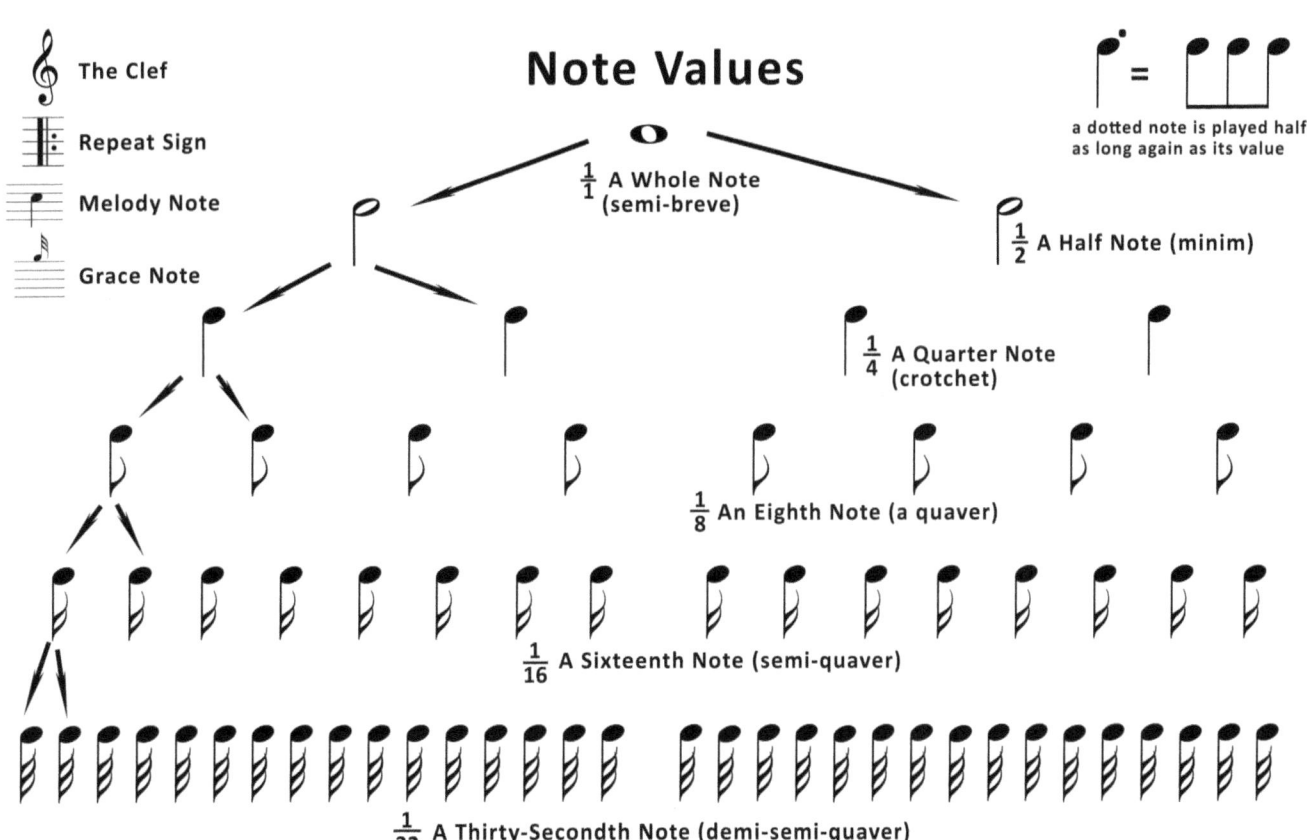

Learn the Highland Bagpipe - first steps for absolute beginners

Fingering on the Practice Chanter

"App – Videos – Basic Exercises 1 – Fingering on the Practice Chanter"

Look at these pictures to see how your fingers should be placed on the practice chanter. It's usual practice to have your left hand above your right, but some students find it easier the other way around – and if right above left is more comfortable for you, no problem! Start by placing your right hand fingers on the lower four fingerholes.

1. Right hand – place the upper pad of your pinkie on the lowest fingerhole **(Low A finger)**.

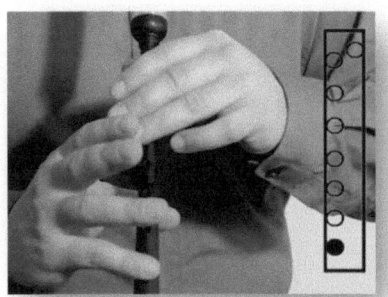

2. Right hand – place the middle pad of your ring finger over the second lowest fingerhole **(B finger)**.

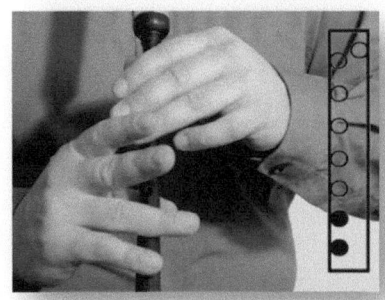

3. Right hand – place the middle pad of your middle finger over the third lowest fingerhole **(C finger)**.

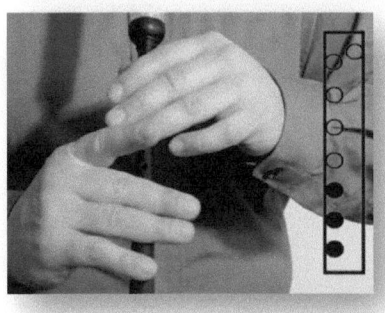

4. Right hand – place the middle pad of your index finger over the fourth lowest fingerhole **(D finger)**.

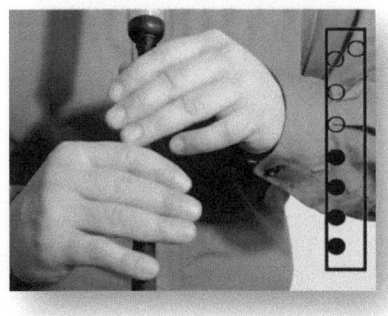

Your right thumb should be positioned on the back of the chanter at a height between the index and middle fingers – apply only light pressure.

OK, your lower (right) hand is on the chanter, now let's position the left hand.

5. Left hand – place your thumb on the rear fingerhole **(High A finger)**.

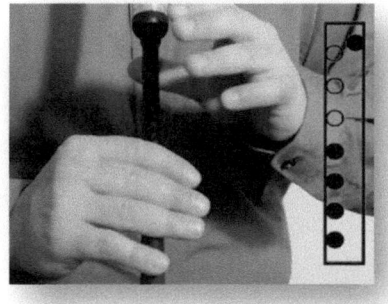

6. Left hand – place the upper or middle pad of your index finger on the highest fingerhole **(High G finger).**

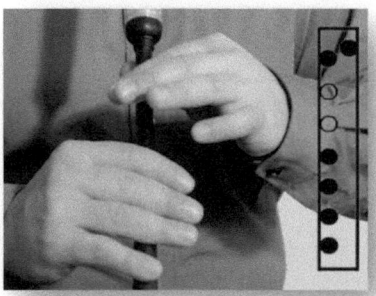

7. Left hand – place the upper or middle pad of your middle finger on the next fingerhole **(F finger)**.

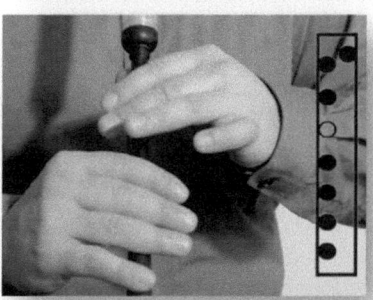

8. Left hand – place the upper pad of your ring finger on the next fingerhole **(E finger)**.

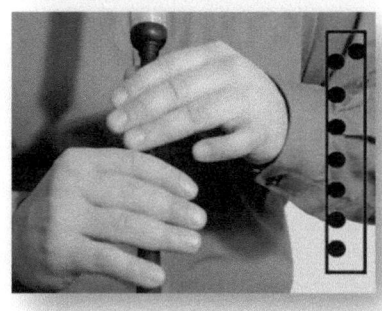

Remember...
Use only gentle pressure on the chanter with your upper and lower thumbs.
All your fingers should be lying straight (stretched but relaxed) on the chanter.

Scales and Exercises

The first note – Low G
Place all your fingers on the chanter as described. Now blow gently into the mouthpiece. The note you're now hearing is the first and lowest note, the

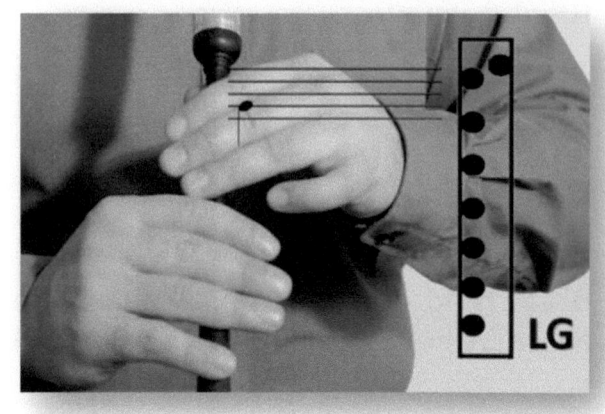

The second note – Low A
Now lift your lower pinkie and blow gently again. This is the

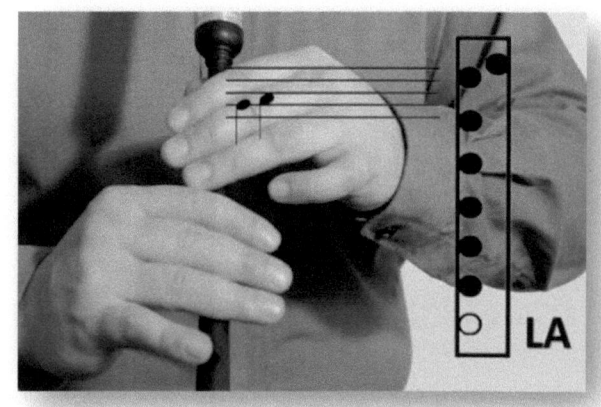

Low G to Low A Scale
"App – Videos – Basic Exercises 1 – Low G to Low A Scale"

Play this exercise a few times, making sure that your fingers are lying straight (stretched but relaxed) on the chanter.

Remember...
Play the notes slowly and evenly.

The third note – B
Now lift your right (hand) ring finger to play the next note. Blow gently into the chanter again.
This is a

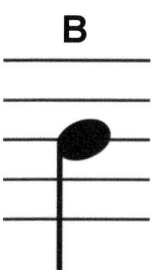

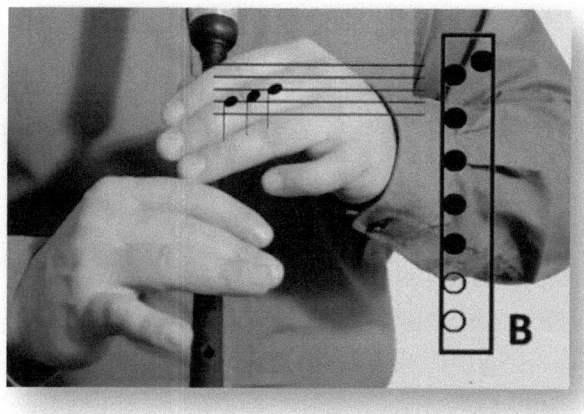

Low G to B Scale
"App – Videos – Basic Exercises 1 – Low G to B Scale"

Play this scale a few times until you're confident your fingering is correct.

The fourth note – C
Lift your right middle finger and at the same time, lower your right pinkie, closing that fingerhole.
This is a

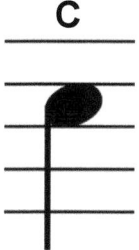

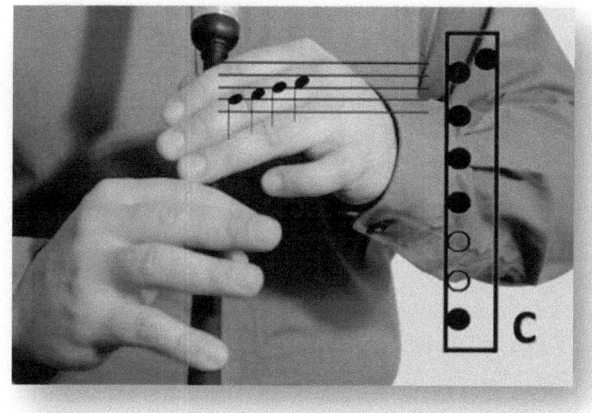

Low G to C Scale
"App – Videos – Basic Exercises 1 – Low G to C Scale"

Play this exercise a few times until the fingering is no problem for you. Make sure the notes sound clean when you're changing fingers.

Low G to C Exercise
"App – Videos – Basic Exercises 1 – Low G to C Exercise"

The fifth note – D
Now lift your right index finger as well, but keep your pinkie on its fingerhole.
This is a

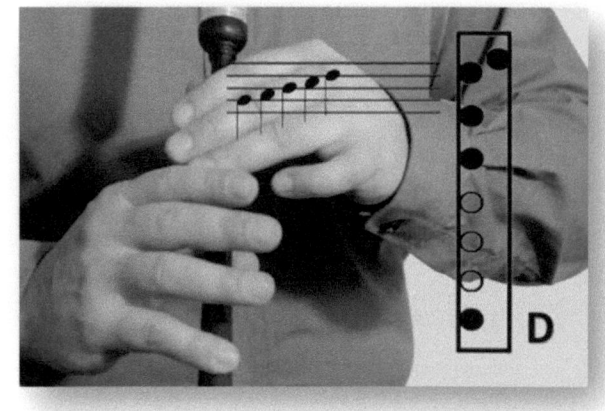

Low G to D Scale
"App – Videos – Basic Exercises 1 – Low G to D Scale"

Low G to D Exercise
"App – Videos – Basic Exercises 1 – Low G to D Exercise"

The sixth note – E
Now it's time to change hands! To do this, place the ring, middle and index fingers of your right hand on their respective fingerholes.
At the same time, lift the ring finger of your left hand and the pinkie of your right hand.

This is an

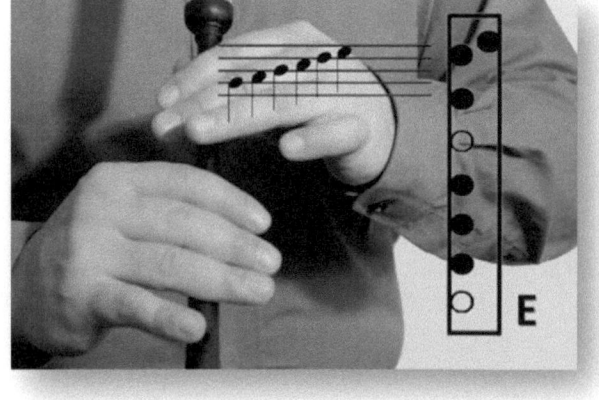

Low G to E Scale
"App – Videos – Basic Exercises 1 – Low G to E Scale"

Low G to E Exercise & D to E Exercise
"App – Videos – Basic Exercises 1 – Low G to E Exercise"

"App – Videos – Basic Exercises 1 – D to E Exercise"

Play these three exercises several times through. Make sure your hand changes are clean. When you're changing notes, try to avoid "crossing noises". Crossing noises are small sounds that are heard when you change notes.

The seventh note – F
Lift your left middle finger to get to the next note.
Leave your lower hand as is on the chanter.
This is an

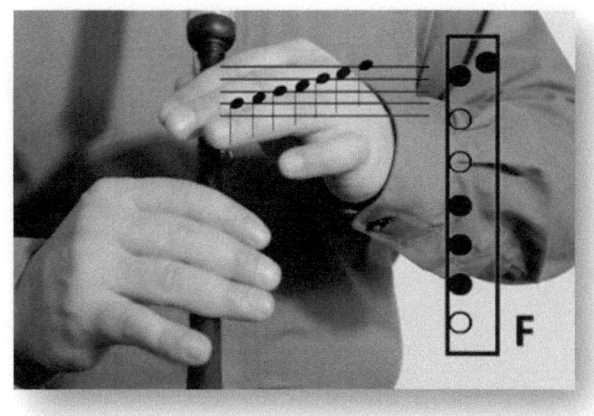

Low G to F Scale
"App – Videos – Basic Exercises 1 – Low G to F Scale"

You should only continue with the next exercise when you can play all the previous ones accurately.

Low G to F Exercise
"App – Videos – Basic Exercises 1 – Low G to F Exercise"

The eighth note – High G

Lift your left index finger. Make sure that your left index, middle and ring fingers don't stray too far up from the chanter. This is a

High G

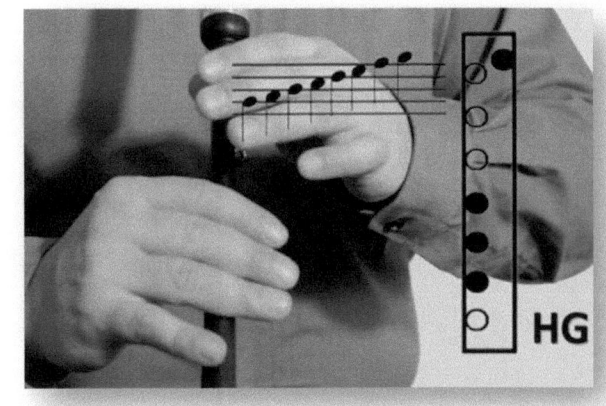

Low G to High G Scale
"App – Videos – Basic Exercises 1 – Low G to High G Scale"

Low G to High G Exercise
"App – Videos – Basic Exercises 1 – Low G to High G Exercise"

The ninth note – High A

Now lower your left ring finger back on to the fingerhole and lift your left thumb at the same time. This is the

High A

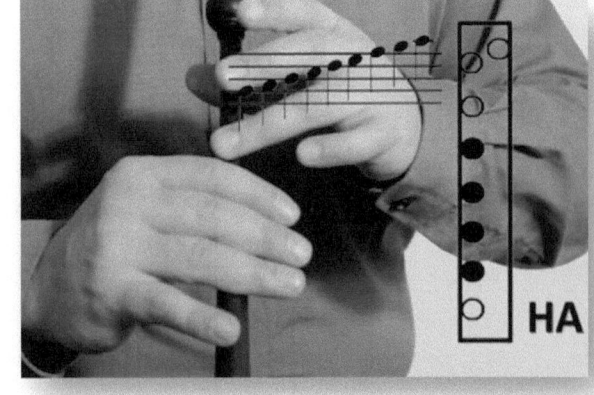

Low G to High A Scale (Complete Scale)
"App – Videos – Basic Exercises 1 – Low G to High A Scale"

Low G to High A Exercise
"App – Videos – Basic Exercises 1 – Low G to High A Exercise"

E to High A exercise

High G to High A exercise

Write down *all* the exercises you've learned in your music book. Always start by drawing the bar lines to divide the space in the staff correctly.

Practise the finger exercises you've learned slowly and smoothly. Set a metronome at slow speed to help you and play one melody note per beat.

Only go on to the next page if you're confident that you can play all the exercises correctly.

> ### Remember...
> From now on, NO LOOKING AT YOUR FINGERS!
> Always hold the practice chanter loosely in your fingers – don't tighten up!
> And practise every day!

Play the following note **change exercises** as often as you can for several days – and focus on what you've learned.

"App – Videos – Basic Exercises 2 – Changing Exercise 1 - 7"

First play all the notes on the lines.

Now play the notes in the spaces between the lines.

This is the "big jumps" exercise. Change fingers cleanly, avoiding "crossing noises".

Does this tune sound familiar?

Play all the notes on the lines again.

Change notes cleanly!

This exercise helps your fingers to move precisely.

Congratulations! Now you've learned the complete scale and some important exercises too! You've reached the first milestone on your journey to becoming a good bagpipe player!

Now continue working with the Bagpipe Tutorial book.

the Bagpipe Tutorial book

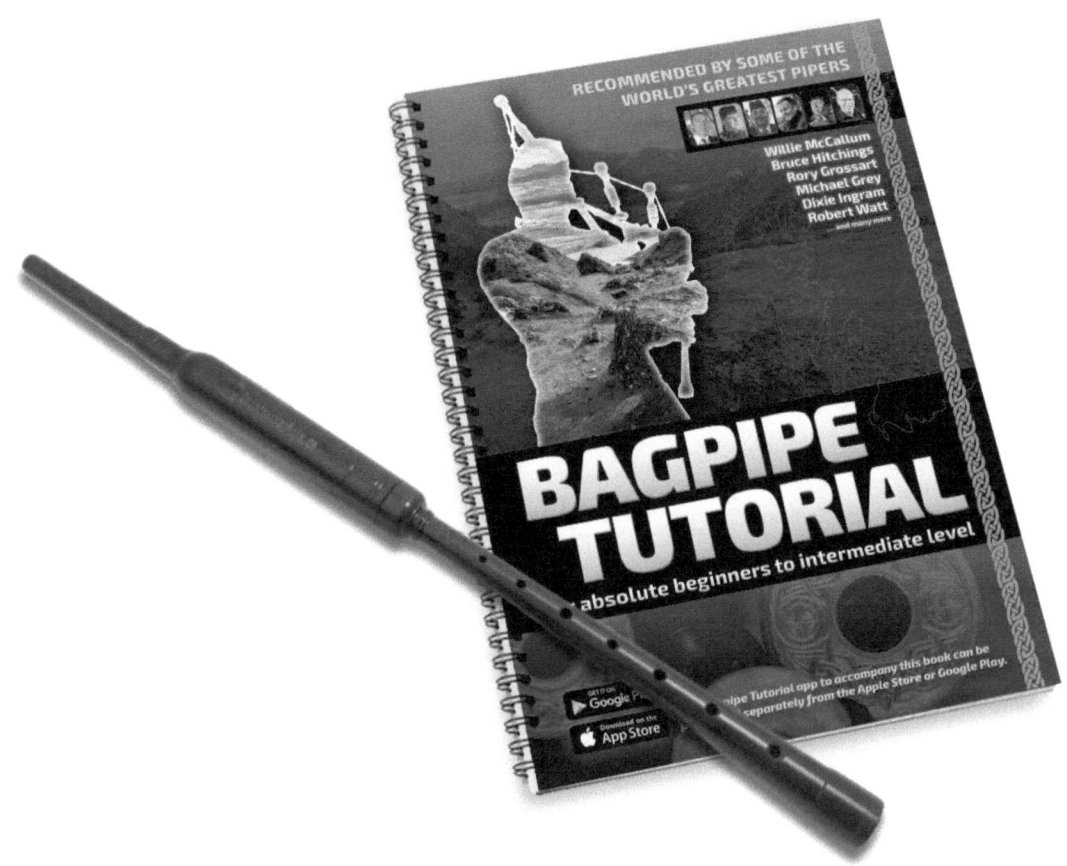

Available from Amazon or **www.bagpipe-tutorial.com**

All Grace Notes, Embellishments and Exercises

App - Video - Basic Exercises 1 - Low G to Low A Scale

App - Video - Basic Exercises 1 - Low G to B Scale

App - Video - Basic Exercises 1 - Low G to C Scale

App - Video - Basic Exercises 1 - Low G to C Exercise

App - Video - Basic Exercises 1 - Low G to D Scale

App - Video - Basic Exercises 1 - Low G to D Exercise

App - Video - Basic Exercises 1 - Low G to E Scale

Learn the Highland Bagpipe - first steps for absolute beginners

App - Video - Basic Exercises 1 - Low G to E Exercise

App - Video - Basic Exercises 1 - D to E Exercise

App - Video - Basic Exercises 1 - Low G to F Scale

App - Video - Basic Exercises 1 - Low G to F Exercise

App - Video - Basic Exercises 1 - Low G to High G Scale

App - Video - Basic Exercises 1 - Low G to High G Exercise

App - Video - Basic Exercises 1 - Low G to High A Scale

App - Video - Basic Exercises 1 - Low G to High A Exercise

App - Videos - Basic Exercises 2 - Changing Exercise 1

App - Videos - Basic Exercises 2 - Changing Exercise 2

App - Videos - Basic Exercises 2 - Changing Exercise 3

App - Videos - Basic Exercises 2 - Changing Exercise 4

App - Videos - Basic Exercises 2 - Changing Exercise 5

App - Videos - Basic Exercises 2 - Changing Exercise 6

App - Videos - Basic Exercises 2 - Changing Exercise 7

App - Basic Exercises 2 - Crossing Noise Exercise High A

App - Basic Exercises 2 - Crossing Noise Exercise High G

App - Basic Exercises 2 - Crossing Noise Exercise F

App - Basic Exercises 2 - Crossing Noise Exercise E

App - Basic Exercises 2 - Crossing Noise Exercise D

App - Basic Exercises 2 - Crossing Noise Exercise C

App - Basic Exercises 2 - Crossing Noise Exercise B

App - Basic Exercises 2 - Crossing Noise Exercise Low A

Learn the Highland Bagpipe - first steps for absolute beginners

App - Videos - Single Grace Notes - D - Grace Note Scale

App - Videos - Single Grace Notes - E - Grace Note Scale

App - Videos - Single Grace Notes - F - Grace Note Scale

App - Videos - Single Grace Notes - High G - Grace Note Scale

App - Videos - Single Grace Notes - High A - Grace Note Scale

App - Videos - Single Grace Notes - Tsunami - Scale

App - Videos - Single Grace Notes - G-D-E Exercise 1

App - Videos - Single Grace Notes - G-D-E Exercise 2

App - Videos - Single Grace Notes - G-D-E Exercise 3

Learn the Highland Bagpipe - first steps for absolute beginners

App - Videos - Single Grace Notes - G-D-E Exercise 4

App - Videos - Single Grace Notes - G-D-E Exercise 5

Lesson 20 - G-D-E Single Grace Note Jumps to Low G

Lesson 20 - G-D-E Single Grace Note Jumps to Low A

Lesson 20 - G-D-E Single Grace Note Jumps to B

Lesson 20 - G-D-E Single Grace Note Jumps to C

Additional G-D-E Jumps

Additional G-D-E Jumps

Additional G-D-E Jumps

Learn the Highland Bagpipe - first steps for absolute beginners

App - Videos - Doublings - Double High A

App - Videos - Doublings - Double High G

App - Videos - Doublings - Double F

App - Videos - Doublings - Double E

App - Videos - Doublings - Double D

App - Videos - Doublings - Double C

App - Videos - Doublings - Double B

App - Videos - Doublings - Double Low A

App - Videos - Doublings - Double Low G

Doubling Scale

Learn the Highland Bagpipe - first steps for absolute beginners

App - Videos - Embellishments - Throw on D Style 1

App - Videos - Embellishments - Throw on D Style 2

App - Videos - Embellishments - Grip

App - Videos - Embellishments - Double Catch on B

App - Videos - Embellishments - Double Catch on C

App - Videos - Embellishments - Taorluath

App - Videos - Embellishments - Taorluath on Low A

App - Videos - Embellishments - Birl

Learn the Highland Bagpipe - first steps for absolute beginners

App - Videos - Embellishments - G - Grace Note Birl

App - Videos - Embellishments - Half Strikes

App - Videos - Embellishments - Strikes

App - Videos - Embellishments - Double Strikes

App - Videos - Embellishments - Tachums

App - Videos - Embellishments - Double Tachums

App - Videos - Embellishments - Rodin

App - Videos - Embellishments - Darado - Bubbly Note

Copyright © bagpipe-tutorial.com

Learn the Highland Bagpipe - first steps for absolute beginners

App - Videos - Piobaireachd - Taorluath Amach

App - Videos - Piobaireachd - Crunluath

App - Videos - Piobaireachd - Crunluath Breabach

App - Videos - Piobaireachd - Crunluath Amach

App - Videos - Piobaireachd - Crunluath Fosgailte

Learn the Highland Bagpipe - first steps for absolute beginners

App - Videos - Piobaireachd - Dre

App - Videos - Piobaireachd - Dare

App - Videos - Piobaireachd - Chedare

App - Videos - Piobaireachd - Bari

App - Videos - Piobaireachd - Adeda

App - Videos - Piobaireachd - Harin

App - Videos - Piobaireachd - Double Echos

Learn the Highland Bagpipe - first steps for absolute beginners

App - Videos - More Exercises - Strathspey Triplets

App - Videos - More Exercises - 6/8-Movements

App - Videos - More Exercises - Strathspey Double Tachums 1

App - Videos - More Exercises - Strathspey Double Tachums 2

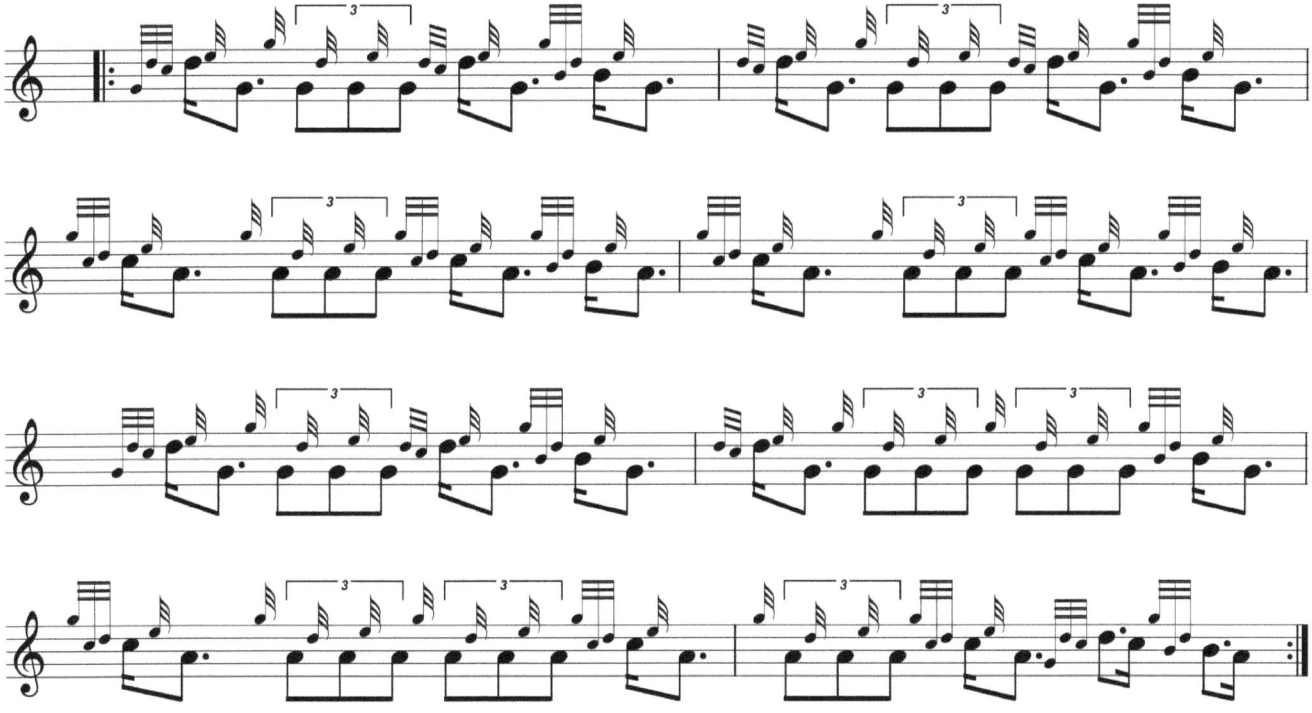

App - Videos - More Exercises - D - Grace Note Tachum Variation

Learn the Highland Bagpipe - first steps for absolute beginners

App - Videos - More Exercises - Fast Finger Exercise High A

App - Videos - More Exercises - Fast Finger Exercise High G

App - Videos - More Exercises - Fast Finger Exercise F

App - Videos - More Exercises - Fast Finger Exercise E

App - Videos - More Exercises - Fast Finger Exercise D

App - Videos - More Exercises - Fast Finger Exercise C

App - Videos - More Exercises - Fast Finger Exercise B

App - Videos - More Exercises - Fast Finger Exercise Low A

App - Videos - More Exercises - Fast Finger Exercise Low G